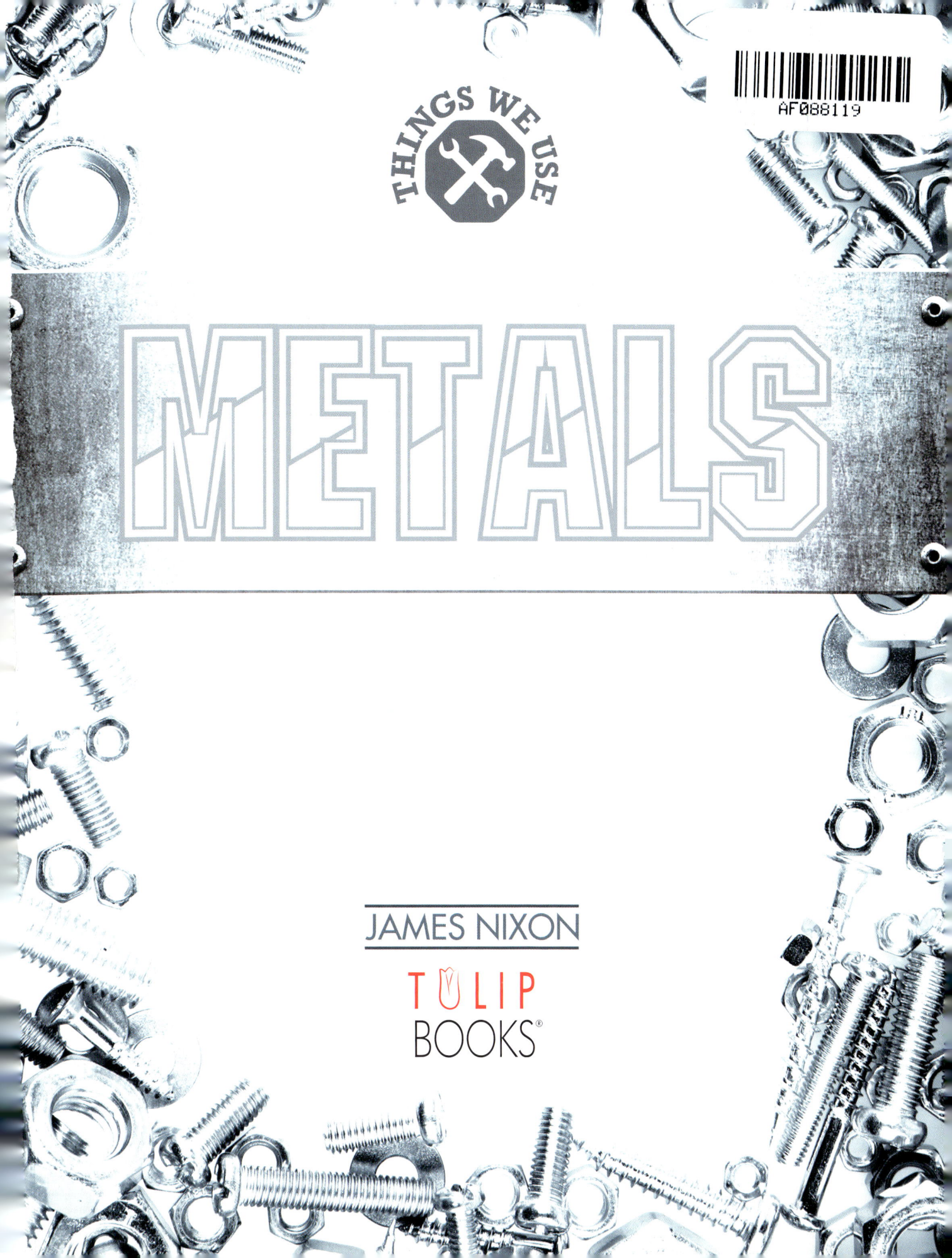
THINGS WE USE
METALS

JAMES NIXON

TULIP BOOKS

Tulip Books Limited

© 2019 Tulip Books Limited

Tulip Books
Suite LP33738
20-22 Wenlock Road
London N1 7GU

Series designed by Jurian Wiese
Book designed by Keith Williams, sprout.uk.com

Production by Discovery Books

British Library Cataloguing in Publication Data
A full catalogue record for this book is available from the British Library

Picture Credits: Alamy: pp. 8 top (Greenshoots Communications), 18 (Friedrich Stark), 20 (imageBROKER), 21 top (Phil Degginger). FreeImages.com: p. 6–7 background (Jocelito Ribeiro). Getty Images: pp. 9 (Matt Mawson), 15 top (Ullstein Bild). Shutterstock: pp. 4 (Africa Studio), 5 (Ivan Kurmyshov), 6 left (TADDEUS), 6 top right (Elena Schweitzer), 6 bottom right (Praisaeng), 7 top (Koldunov), 7 middle left (Gena96), 7 middle right (Siarhei Dzmitryienka), 7 bottom (Tanya Rozhnovskaya), 8 inset (Salienko Evgenii), 10–11 (Norenko Andrey), 10 inset (Rattanapon Ninlapoom), 12 (PhotoStock10), 12 inset (Michael Allen), 13 top (Syda Productions), 13 bottom (Gines Romero), 14 (Panksvatouny), 14 inset (Aumm graphixphoto), 15 inset (DuxX), 15 bottom (Steve Photography), 16 (Matej Kastelic), 17 (H.Tanaka), 19 top (amophoto_au), 19 bottom (creivei images), 21 inset (FreeProd33), 22 top (DenisNata), 22 bottom (Maximumm).

All the internet addresses (URLs) given in this book were valid at the time of going to press. However, due to the dynamic nature of the internet, some addresses may have changed, or sites may have changed or ceased to exist since publication. While the author and publisher regret any inconvenience this may cause readers, no responsibility for such changes can be accepted by either the author or the publisher.

ISBN 978-1-78388-143-7

All rights reserved. No part of this publication may be reproduced, stored in a retrieval system or transmitted, in any form or by any means, electronic, mechanical, photocopying, recording or otherwise, without the prior permission of Tulip Books Limited.

CONTENTS

What is a metal?	4
How are metals used?	6
Where are metals found?	8
Processing metal	10
Mixing metals	12
Shaping metal	14
Building with metal	16
Metal on the move	18
Recycling metal	20
Metals fact file	22
Glossary	23
Further information	24
Index	24

WHAT IS A METAL?

Metals are hard, natural **materials** found underground in rocks. Metals are very useful to us. You can see metals around you in the things you use every day.

Metals are strong and can be shaped without breaking or cracking. They are used to make thousands of things, from keys and cutlery, to cars and **skyscrapers**.

HOW ARE METALS USED?

Metals are everywhere! See how these different types are used:

Iron is used to make steel. It is hard and strong, and used in many tools.

Wires are made from copper because they are good at carrying **electricity**.

Shiny metals, such as gold and silver, are used to make jewellery.

Heat passes well through aluminium, which is used in cooking pans.

Thin layers of zinc are added to many products because it doesn't **rust**.

Nickel is used to make coins. It is tough and will not wear down.

Stainless steel is made from iron and nickel. It is waterproof and easy to clean.

WHERE ARE METALS FOUND?

Most metals come from the top layer of the Earth called the crust. The metals are found inside rocks called **ores**.

Huge amounts of ore need to be mined (dug out) to find enough metal. The rock is blasted with **explosives** and large trucks carry the ore away.

FAST FACT

Half of the world's gold has come from mines in South Africa.

Most mines are large pits on the Earth's surface. Some mines tunnel underground. Miners search deep for valuable metals, such as gold.

PROCESSING METAL

Once mined, metals must be removed from their ore. First, a machine crushes the ore into small pieces. Another machine finishes the crushing by grinding the ore into fine powder.

Crushed ore

Some metals, such as iron and silver, are separated using heat and **chemicals**. This process is called smelting. The heat removes the rest of the ore leaving the metal behind.

FAST FACT

Many metals are separated by mixing the crushed ore with water and chemicals.

MIXING METALS

By **melting** and mixing metals together, better materials can be made. These mixtures are called **alloys**.

Steel

Steel alloys are made from iron and a substance called **carbon**. Iron is strong, but rusts easily. Steel is much tougher.

Brass

Brass is a mixture of copper and zinc

Aluminium alloy

Pure aluminium is softer than many metals. However, alloys made from aluminium are strong, but very light.

FAST FACT

Mixing nickel and titanium makes a special alloy called nitinol. Nitinol can be gently bent into shape, and is perfect to use in the frames of glasses.

SHAPING METAL

Metals can be melted at great heat and poured into hollow **moulds**. When the metal cools, it turns into a **solid**, in the shape of the mould.

Hammer

In factories, metals can be hammered, pressed or rolled into shape.

Metals are cut into a final shape using drilling, cutting and grinding machines.

Metal products are usually made in factories, but some are made by hand.

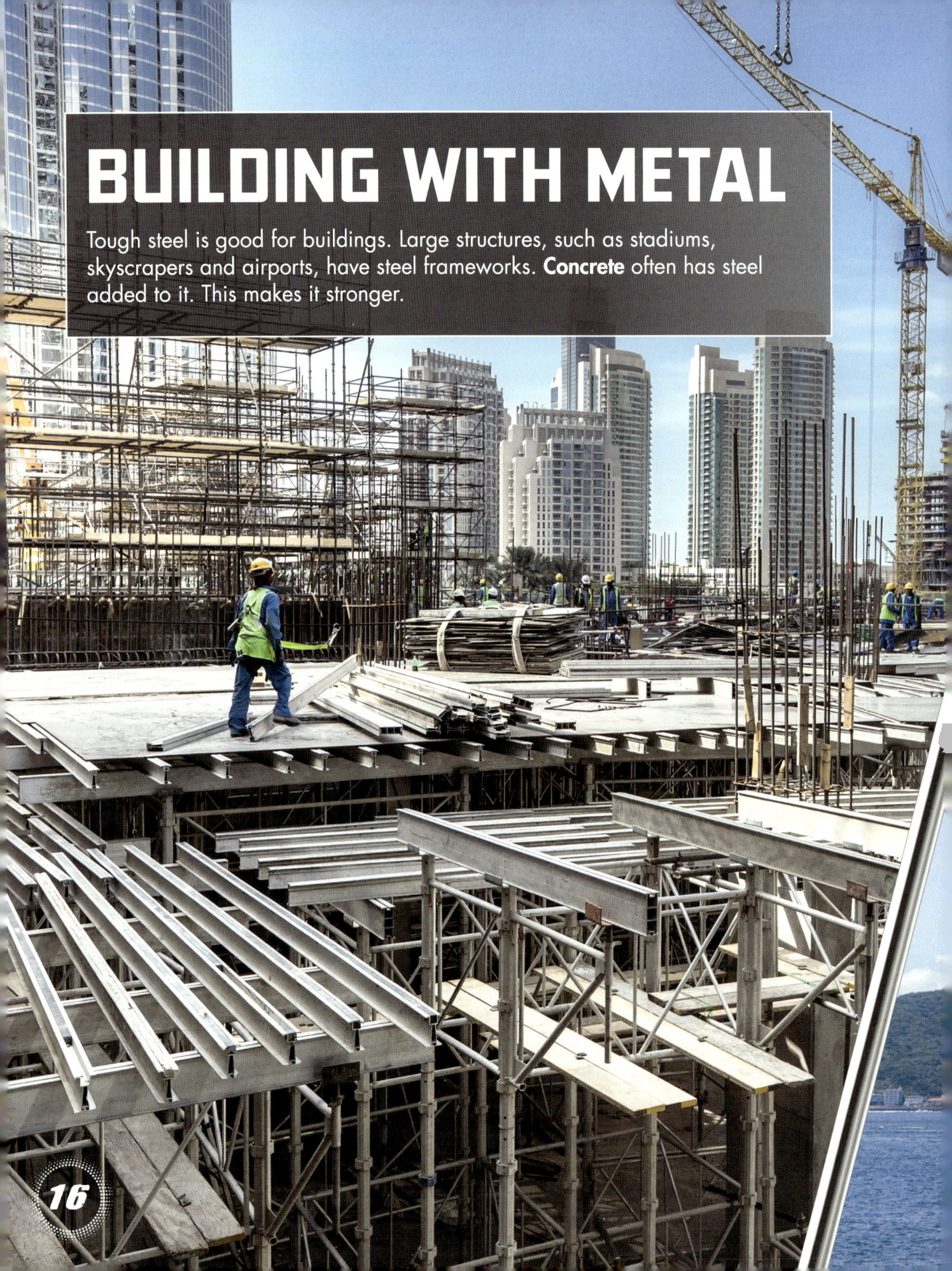

BUILDING WITH METAL

Tough steel is good for buildings. Large structures, such as stadiums, skyscrapers and airports, have steel frameworks. **Concrete** often has steel added to it. This makes it stronger.

Steel is used to make bridges. Huge road bridges are held up by long, steel cables.

FAST FACT

The Akashi Kaikyo Bridge in Japan is nearly 2,000 metres long. The steel cables used would circle the world seven times!

METAL ON THE MOVE

A car is made from lots of different metals. Steel is shaped to make the panels on the bodywork. Steel parts can be easily put together by melting them where they join. This is called welding.

FAST FACT

Steel makes up around 60% of a car's weight.

Steel is used in shipbuilding, too.

Aeroplanes and high-speed trains are made from aluminium, because it is lighter than steel.

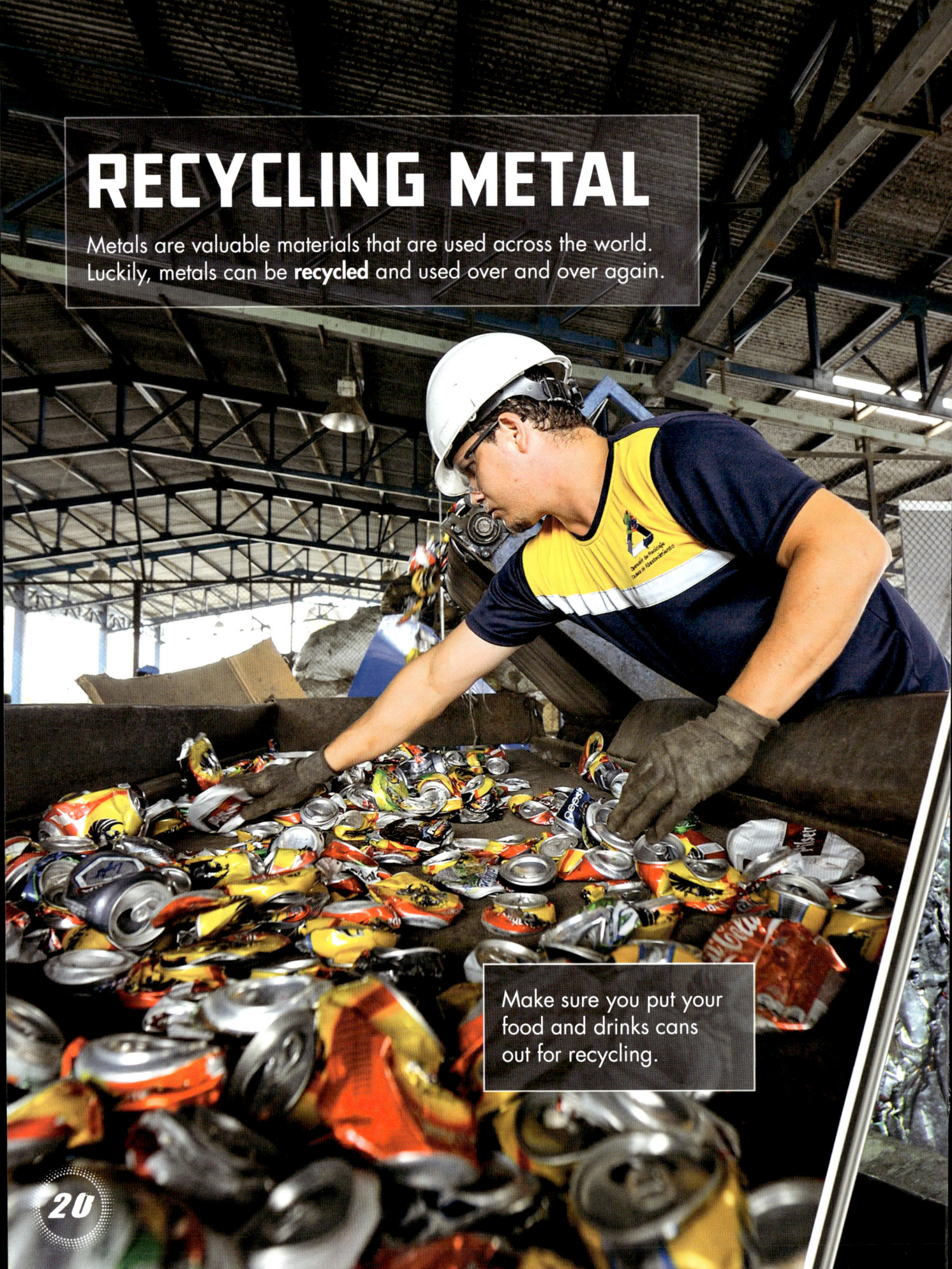

RECYCLING METAL

Metals are valuable materials that are used across the world. Luckily, metals can be **recycled** and used over and over again.

Make sure you put your food and drinks cans out for recycling.

FAST FACT

A recycled aluminium can can be back in the shops in just six weeks!

Recycled cans are melted down and cleaned. The metal is then made into bars of solid metal, ready for use again.

METALS FACT FILE

Steel can be 1,000 times stronger than iron in its pure form.

At **room temperature**, mercury is the only metal that is liquid. It is used inside **thermometers**.

Aluminium is the most common metal found in the Earth's crust.

We use metals to make music. They make a ringing sound when they are hit.

GLOSSARY

alloy a mixture of two or more metals

carbon a very common material that is not metal. It is found in coal and oil.

chemical a substance used in chemistry

concrete a hard building material made from a mixture of sand, gravel, cement and water

electricity a source of energy that can flow through wires and power many of the gadgets in our home

explosives materials that can be made to blow apart with great force and noise. Explosions can break up rock at mine sites

materials substances used to make things including glass, metal, wood and plastic

melting turning something from a solid to a liquid using heat

mould a hollow shape that a liquid material can be poured into. The material cools and hardens into the shape of the mould

ore a rock that contains a useful material, such as a metal

recycled used again instead of being thrown away

room temperature about 20 degrees Celsius, the normal temperature inside a house

rust a brown or orange stain that forms on a metal and weakens it. It forms when the metal is exposed to air or water

skyscraper a very tall building

solid a solid material has a fixed shape, unlike a liquid

thermometer a tool used to measure the temperature of something. Mercury rises and falls inside the glass tube as the temperature changes

FURTHER INFORMATION

Books
Metal (Exploring Materials), Abby Colich, Raintree, 2014

Metal (What Happens When We Recycle?), Jillian Powell, Franklin Watts, 2014

Metal (Materials), Harriet Brundle, BookLife Publishing, 2017

Websites
Videos, facts, quizzes and much more about metals can be found on this website:
http://www.sciencekids.co.nz/metals.html
Here, you can take a closer look at iron and steel:
https://www.explainthatstuff.com/ironsteel.html

INDEX

aeroplanes 19
alloys 12, 13
aluminium 7, 13, 19, 21, 22

brass 12
bridges 17
buildings 16

cans 20, 21
carbon 12
cars 5, 18
chemicals 11
coins 7
concrete 16
copper 6, 12
cutlery 5
cutting metals 15

factories 15
gold 6, 9
hammering metals 15
iron 6, 7, 12, 22
jewellery 6
melting 12, 14, 18, 21
mercury 22
mines 8, 9
moulds 14
nickel 7, 13
ores 8, 10, 11
recycling 20–21
rocks 4, 8
rust 7, 12

ships 19
silver 6
skyscrapers 5, 16
smelting 11
steel 6, 7, 12, 16, 17, 18, 19, 22
titanium 13
tools 6
trains 19
welding 18
wires 6
zinc 7, 12